# Contents

# Things you can see in winter

You can see snow.

You can see snowballs.

You can see a snowman.

shovel

You can see a shovel.

You can see sledges.

icicle

You can see **icicles**.

You can see **ice skates**.

You can see hats.

You can see gloves.

You can see holly.

You can see snowploughs.

You can see bare trees.

You can see wreaths.

You can see lights.

You can see hot chocolate.

You can see soup.

# Winter quiz

Which clothes would you wear
in winter?

# The four seasons follow a pattern. Which season comes after winter?

**?**

**summer**

**winter**

**autumn**

# Picture glossary

 **ice skates**

 **icicle**

# Index

Answer to quiz on page 20: hats and coats
Answer to question on page 21: spring

# Notes for teachers and parents

## Before reading

**Building background:** Talk about the seasons of the year. Which season are we in at the moment? Ask children what they would see if they looked out of a window in winter.

## After reading

**Recall and reflect:** Which season is before winter? Which season follows winter? What is the weather like in winter? What is the best thing about winter?

**Sentence knowledge:** Help children count the number of words in each sentence.

**Word knowledge (phonics):** Turn to page 10. Ask children which word starts with /y/. Which word starts with /s/? Which word starts with /i/?

**Word recognition:** Ask children to point to the word *see* on any page. Ask children to find the word *see* on other pages.

## Extending ideas

**Make a snowflake:** Give each child a square of white paper. Fold the paper in half to make a triangle. Fold the triangle in half again to make a smaller triangle. Position the triangle with the point down. Fold in each side towards the point. Cut off the top of the folded paper at an angle. Now cut out large shapes from the sides of the triangle. (Children may need help with cutting as the folded paper is thick.) Ask children to open up the triangle to reveal their snowflakes. While making the snowflakes, ask children to identify shapes.

# In this book

## Topic words
gloves
hats
holly
hot chocolate
ice skates
icicles
lights
shovels
sledges
snow
snowballs
snowmen
snowploughs
soup
trees
wreaths

## Topic
winter

## High-frequency words
a
can
see
you

## Sentence stem
You can see _____.

## Ask children to read these words:
hats p. 11
gloves p. 12
hot chocolate p. 18